My Name is...

:::

RETIRED
since

〰〰〰〰〰

STUDIO OF BOOKS
THE SPACE FOR YOUR MESSAGE

STUDIO
OF BOOKS
THE SPACE FOR YOUR MESSAGE

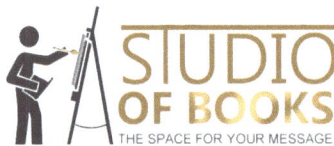

Studio of Books LLC
5900 Balcones Drive Suite 100
Austin, Texas 78731
www.studioofbooks.org
Hotline: (254) 800-1183

Ordering Information:
Special discounts are available on quantity purchases by corporations, associations, and others. For details, contact the publisher at the address above.

Printed in the United States of America.

ISBN-13:   Softcover   978-1-968491-65-9
eBook   978-1-968491-66-6

Library of Congress Control Number:

DEDICATION

I want to dedicate this Journal to my beloved parents Bessie, Lewis Hall, Renchel Lowery. They instilled in me faith, love, Integrity, kindness. I'm forever grateful for their guidance and support.

My Topics

My Retirement Savings

My Employment History
- My Past Employment
- My Pre-Retirement Company
- My First Day on the Job
- My Employer(s) & Supervisors
- My Co-Workers I Liked
- My Co-Workers I Disliked
- My Company Meetings & Events
- My Favorite Office Memories
- My Least Fav Office Memories
- My Raises & Implementations
- My Employer Thoughts of Me
- My Employee Thoughts of Me
- My Day of Retirement

My Retirement Fun
- My Family & Grands
- My Health & Wellness
- My Hobbies
- My Traveling Goals

My Friends & Family, I've Lost

My Special Photos

My Final Words & Reflections

My Retirement Savings

How I Saved For My Retirement

My Employment History

YOU ARE HIRED!

My Past Employment

Names, Years There, Memories, etc.

_____

_____

_____

_____

_____

_____

_____

_____

_____

_____

_____

_____

_____

_____

_____

_____

_____

_____

_____

_____

_____

_____

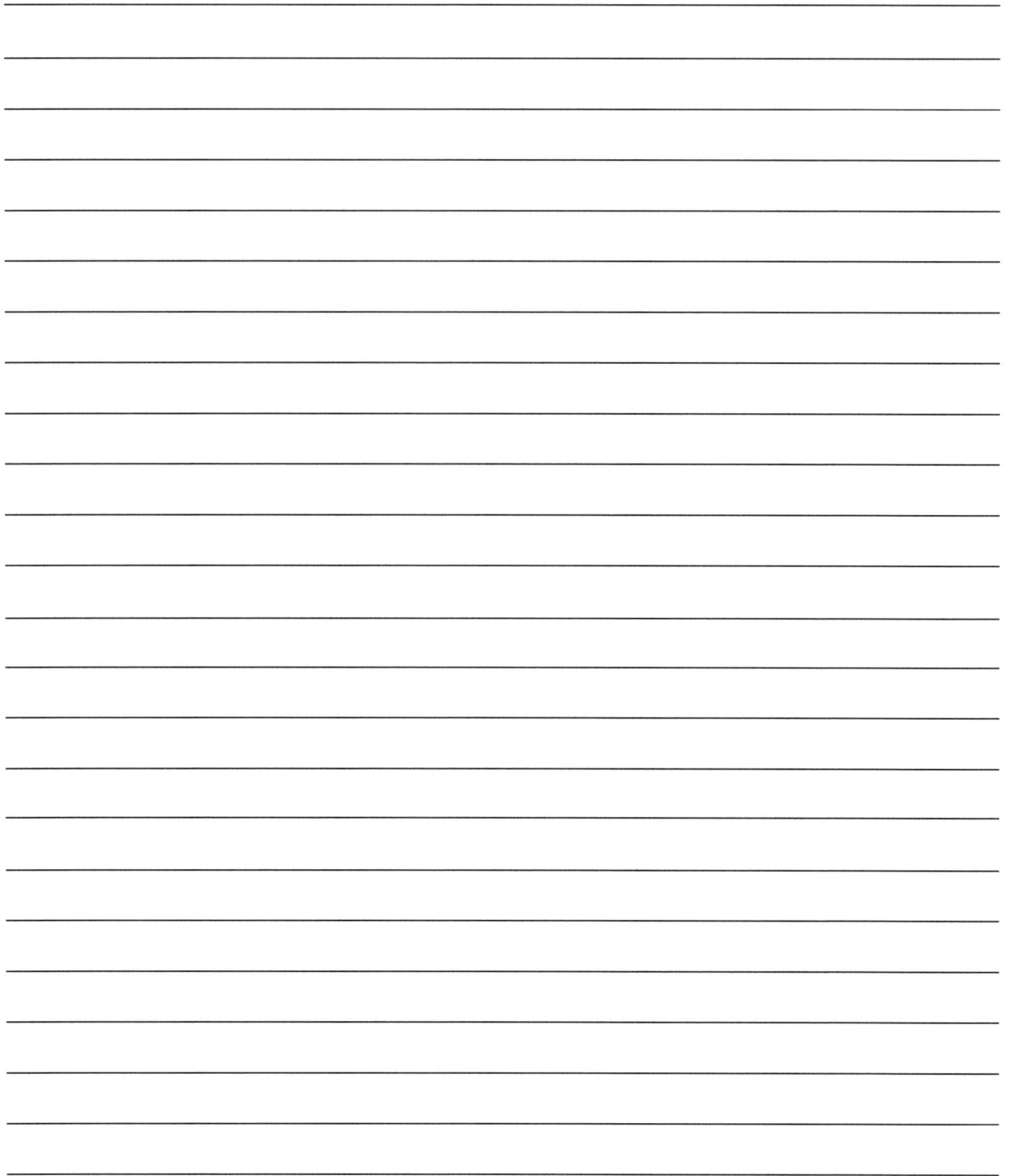

My Pre-Retirement Company

Interview, Name, Purpose, Length There, etc.

_____

_____

_____

_____

_____

_____

_____

_____

_____

_____

_____

_____

_____

_____

_____

_____

_____

_____

_____

_____

_____

_____

My First Day on the Job

Atmosphere, Job Role, Office Decor, etc.

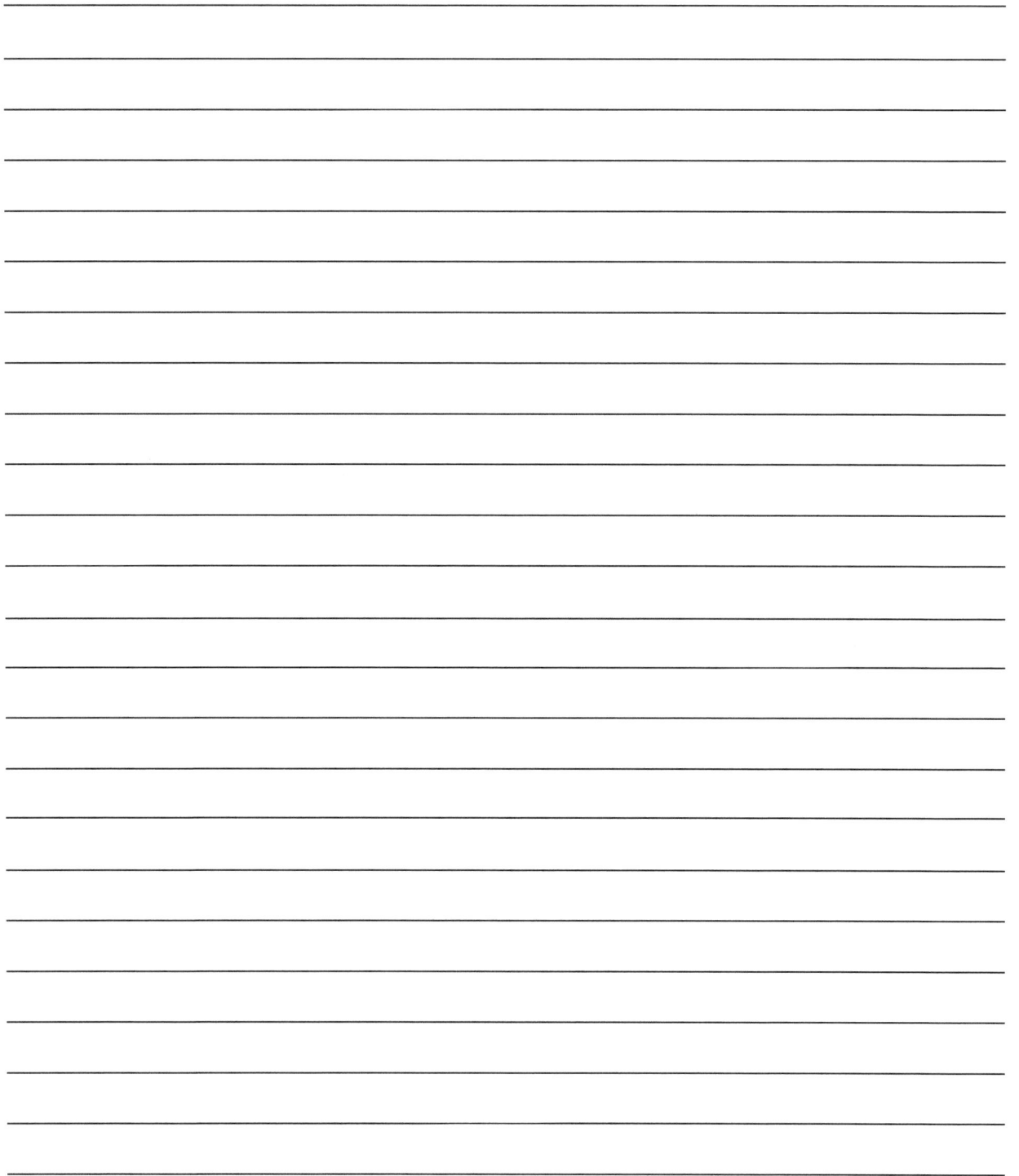

My Employer(s) & Supervisors

Names, How They Made Me Feel, etc.

_____

_____

_____

_____

_____

_____

_____

_____

_____

_____

_____

_____

_____

_____

_____

_____

_____

_____

_____

_____

_____

My Co-Workers I Liked

Explain Why

_____
_____
_____
_____
_____
_____
_____
_____
_____
_____
_____
_____
_____
_____
_____
_____
_____
_____
_____
_____
_____
_____

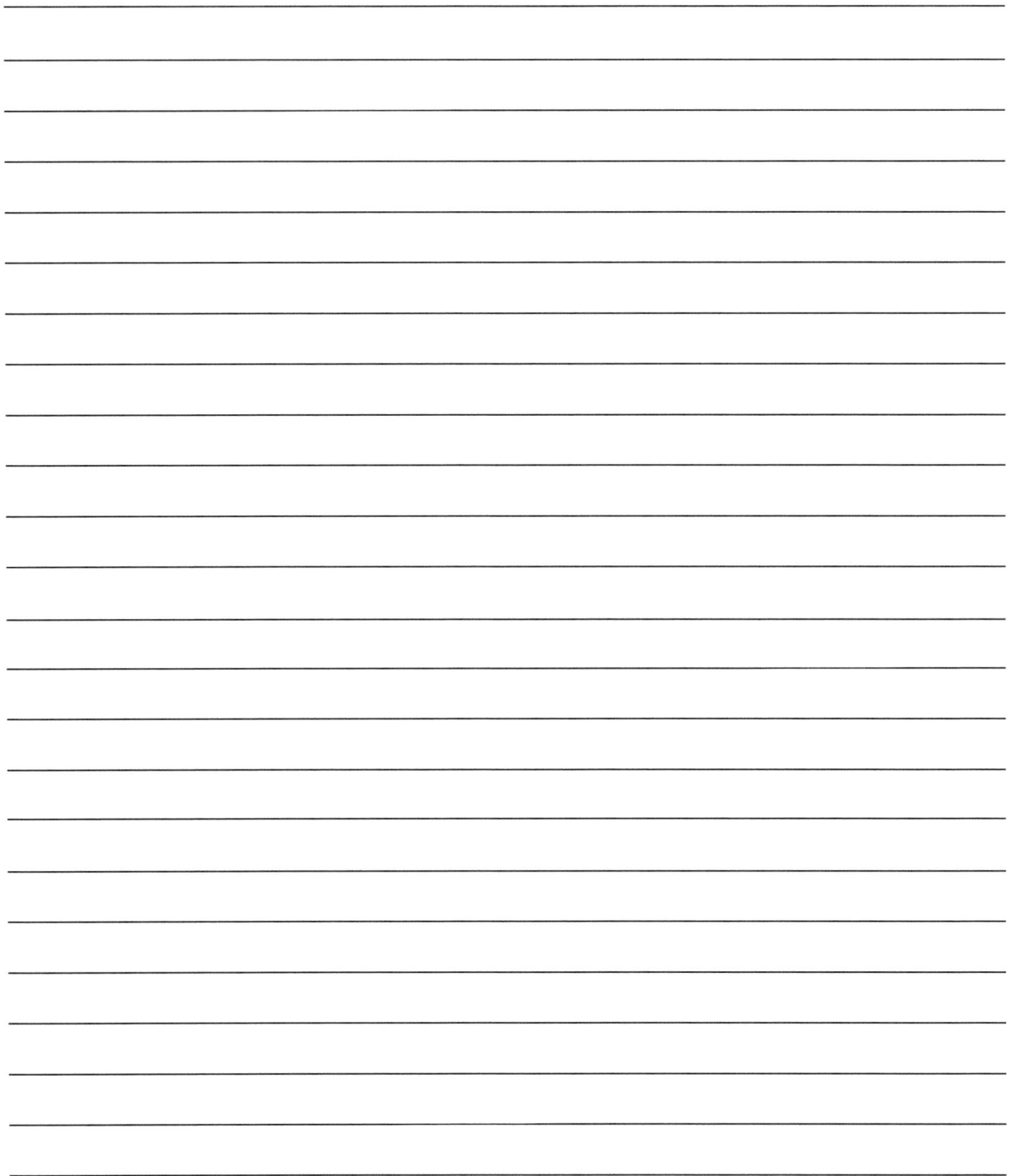

My Co-Workers I Disliked

Explain Why

_____
_____
_____
_____
_____
_____
_____
_____
_____
_____
_____
_____
_____
_____
_____
_____
_____
_____
_____
_____
_____
_____
_____
_____
_____

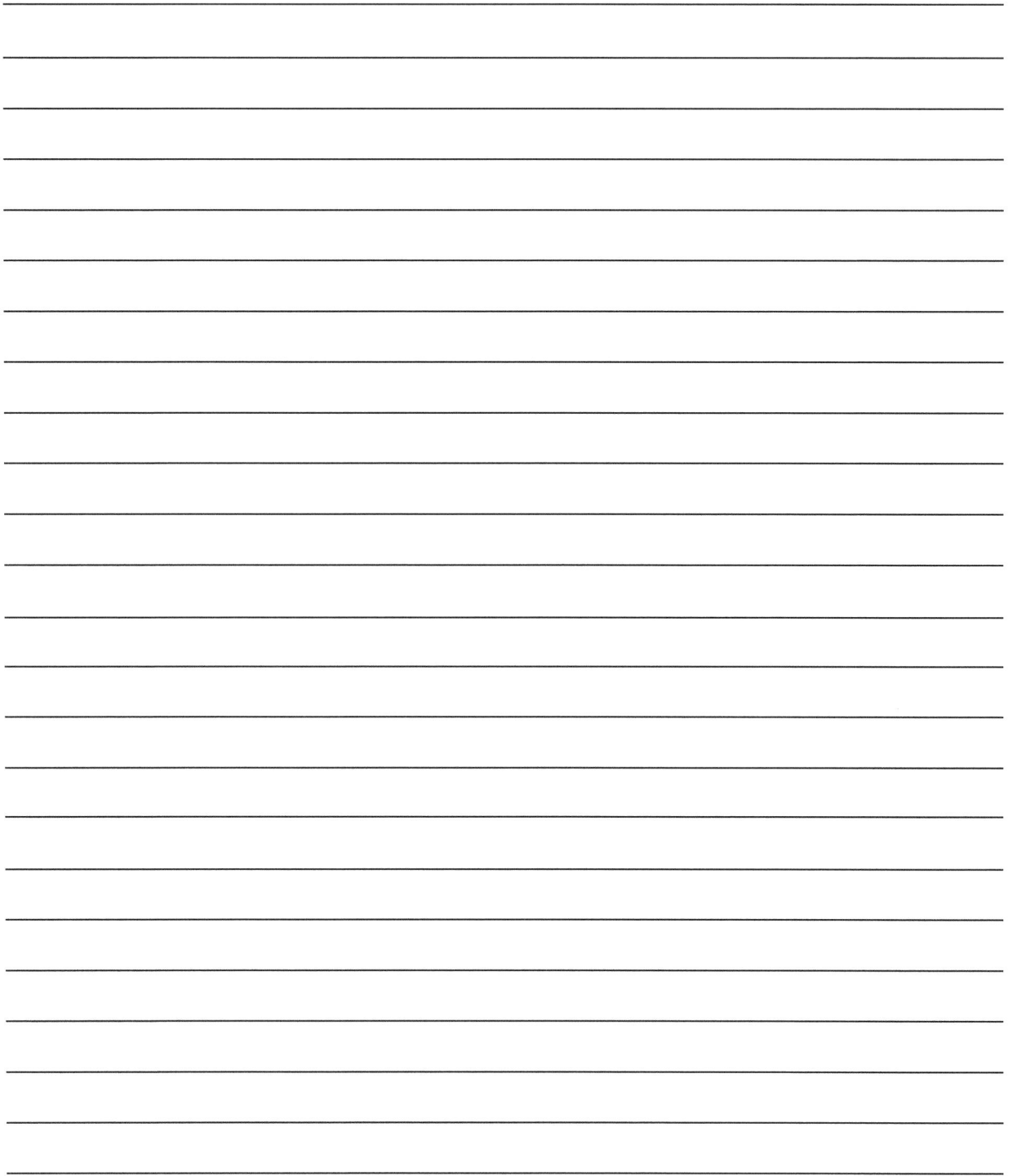

My Company Meetings & Events

Purpose, Details, Holiday Celebrations, etc

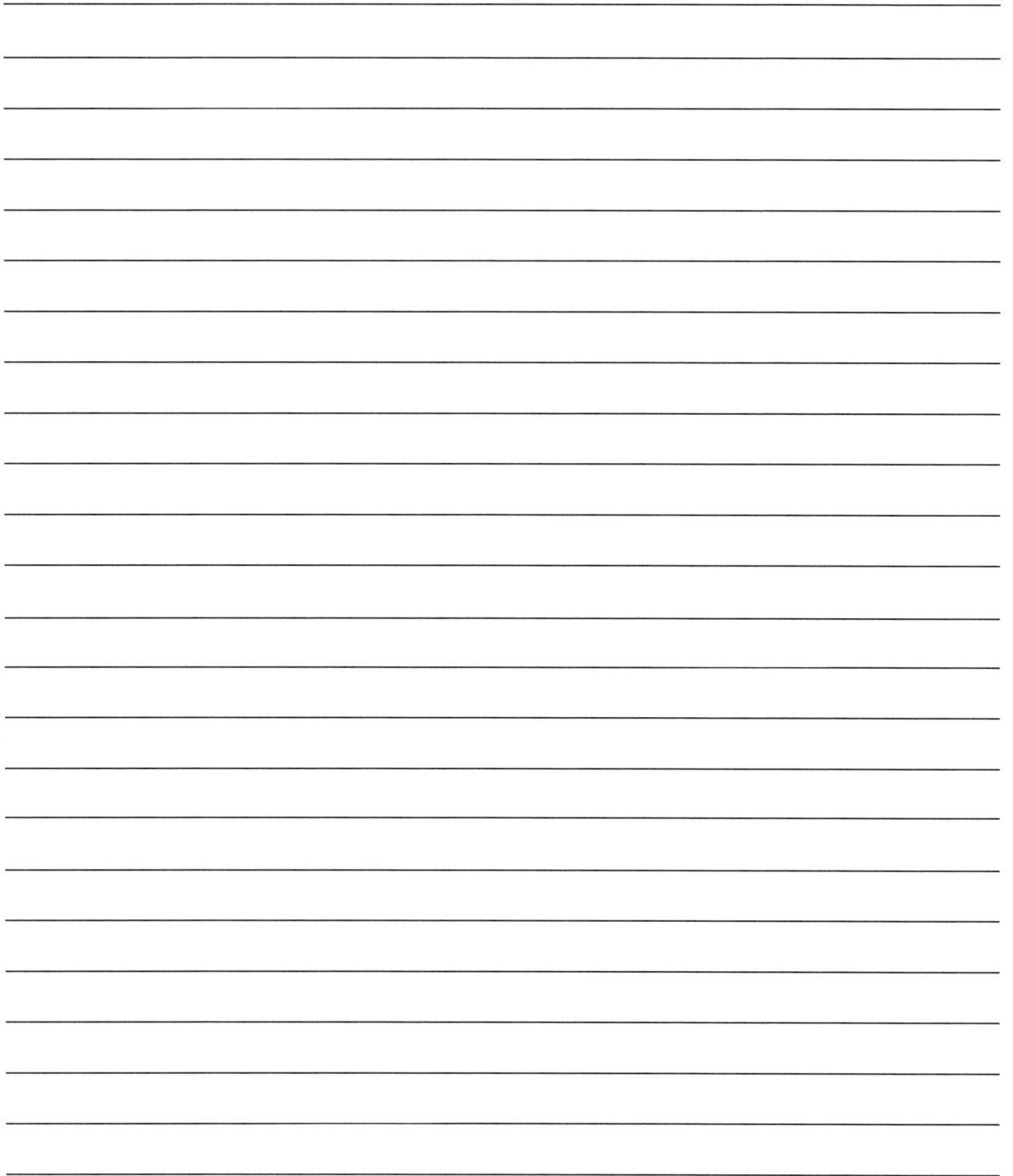

My Favorite Office Memories

What Made Me Happy At Work

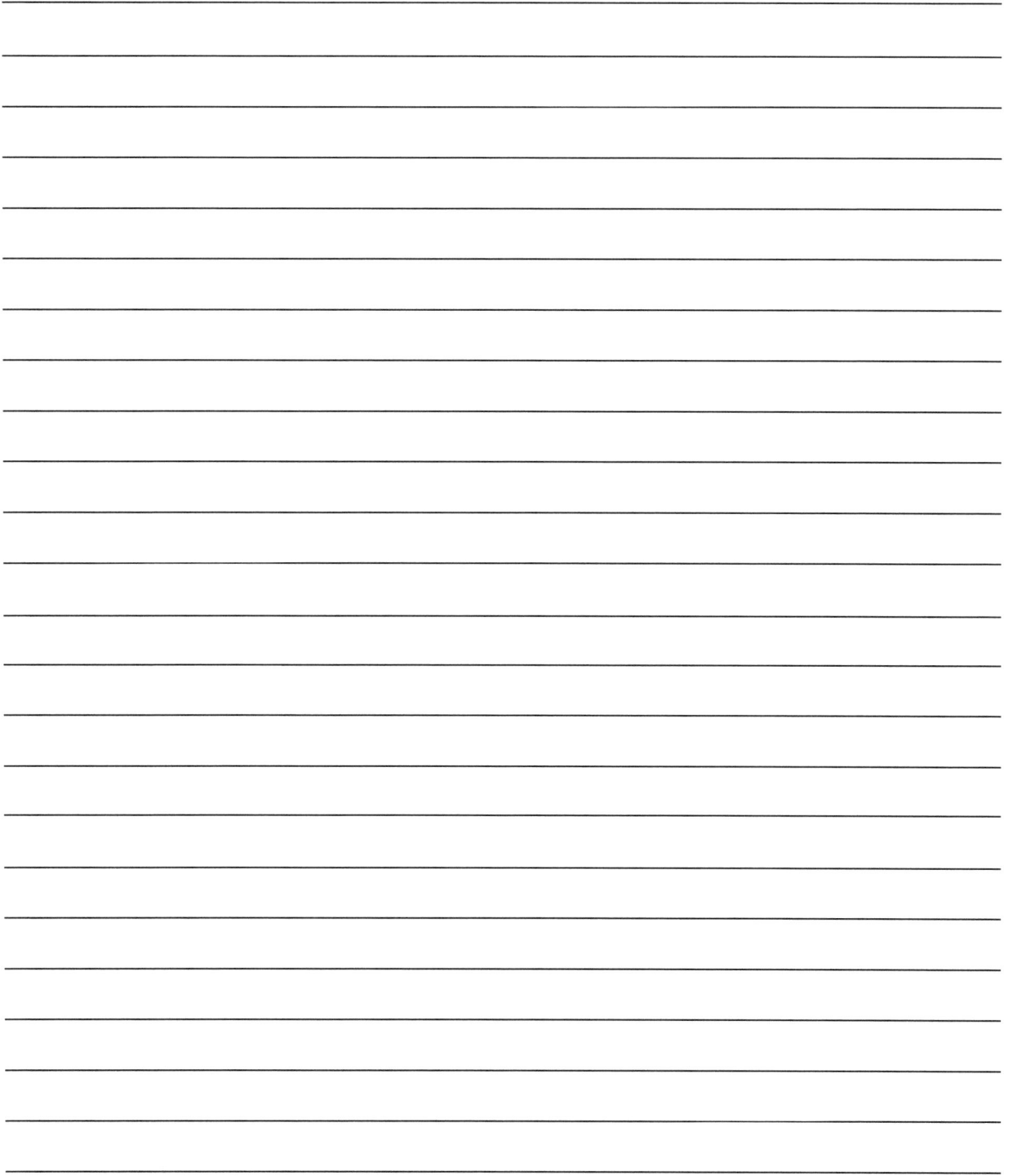

My Least Fav Office Memories

What Made Me Unhappy At Work

_____

_____

_____

_____

_____

_____

_____

_____

_____

_____

_____

_____

_____

_____

_____

_____

_____

_____

_____

_____

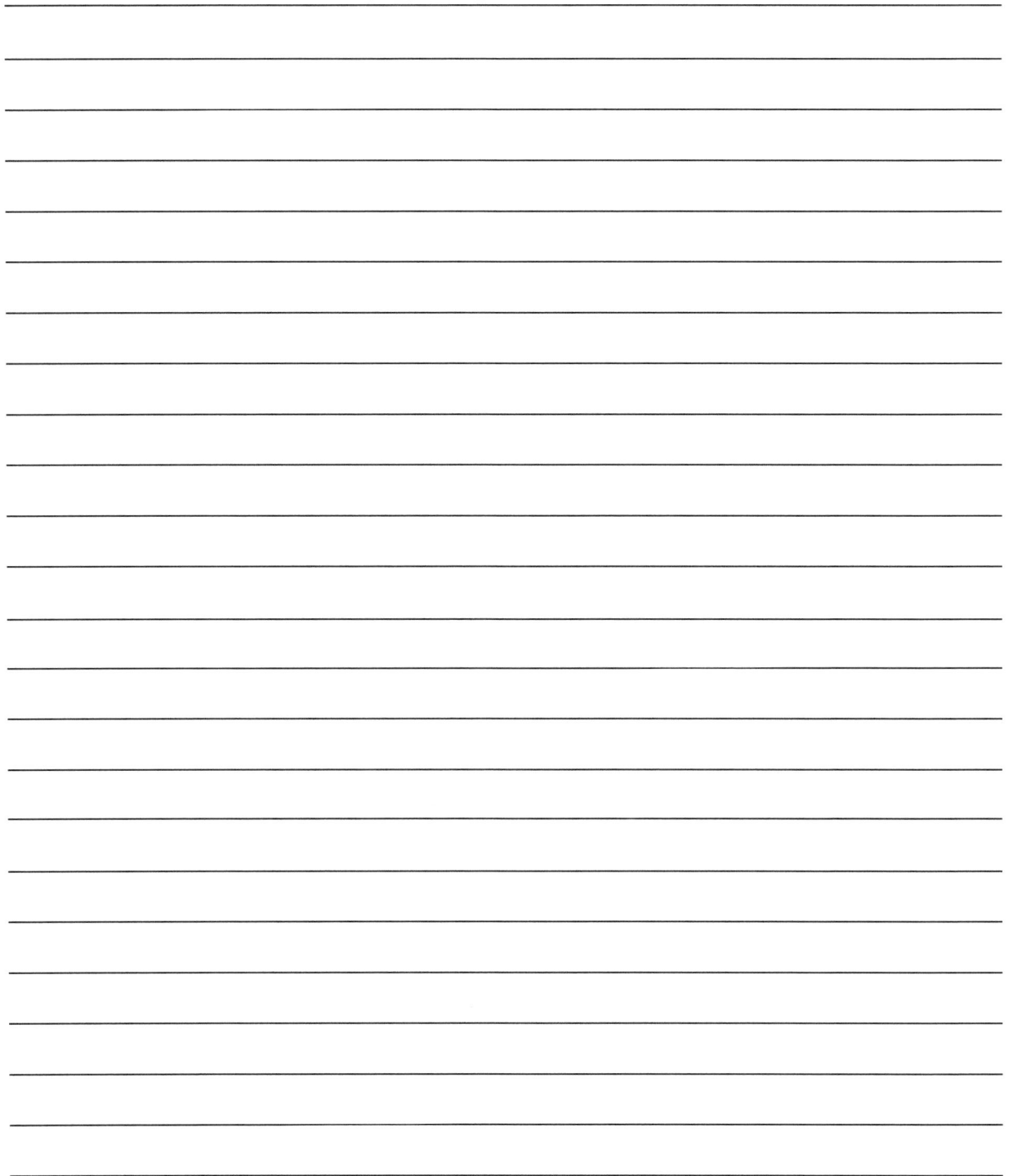

My Raises & Implementations

How I Made A Difference On The Job

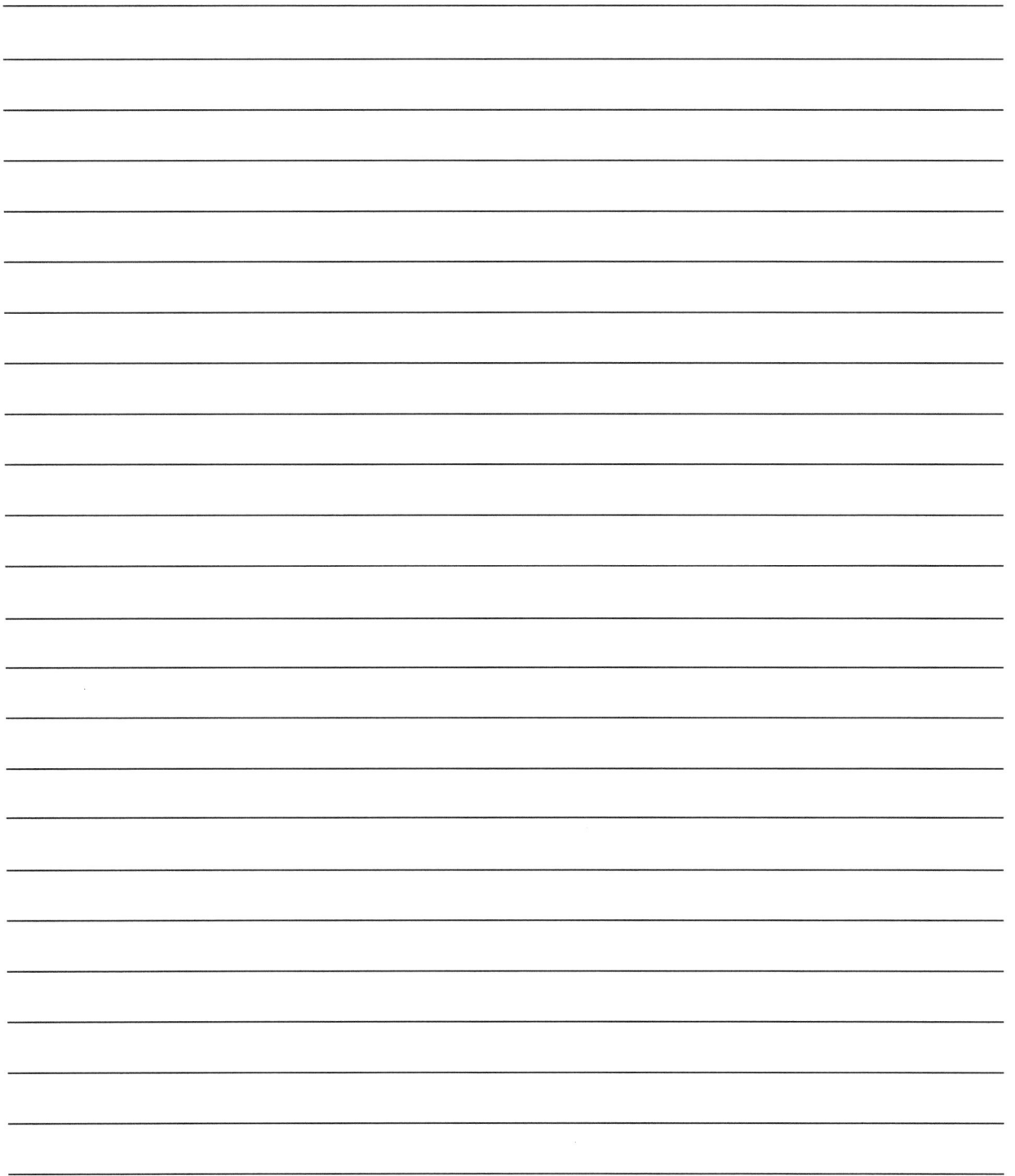

My Employer Thoughts About Me

My Employer Thoughts About Me

My Employee Thoughts About Me

My Employee Thoughts About Me

My Day of Retirement

Recognitions, Celebrations, Gifts, etc.

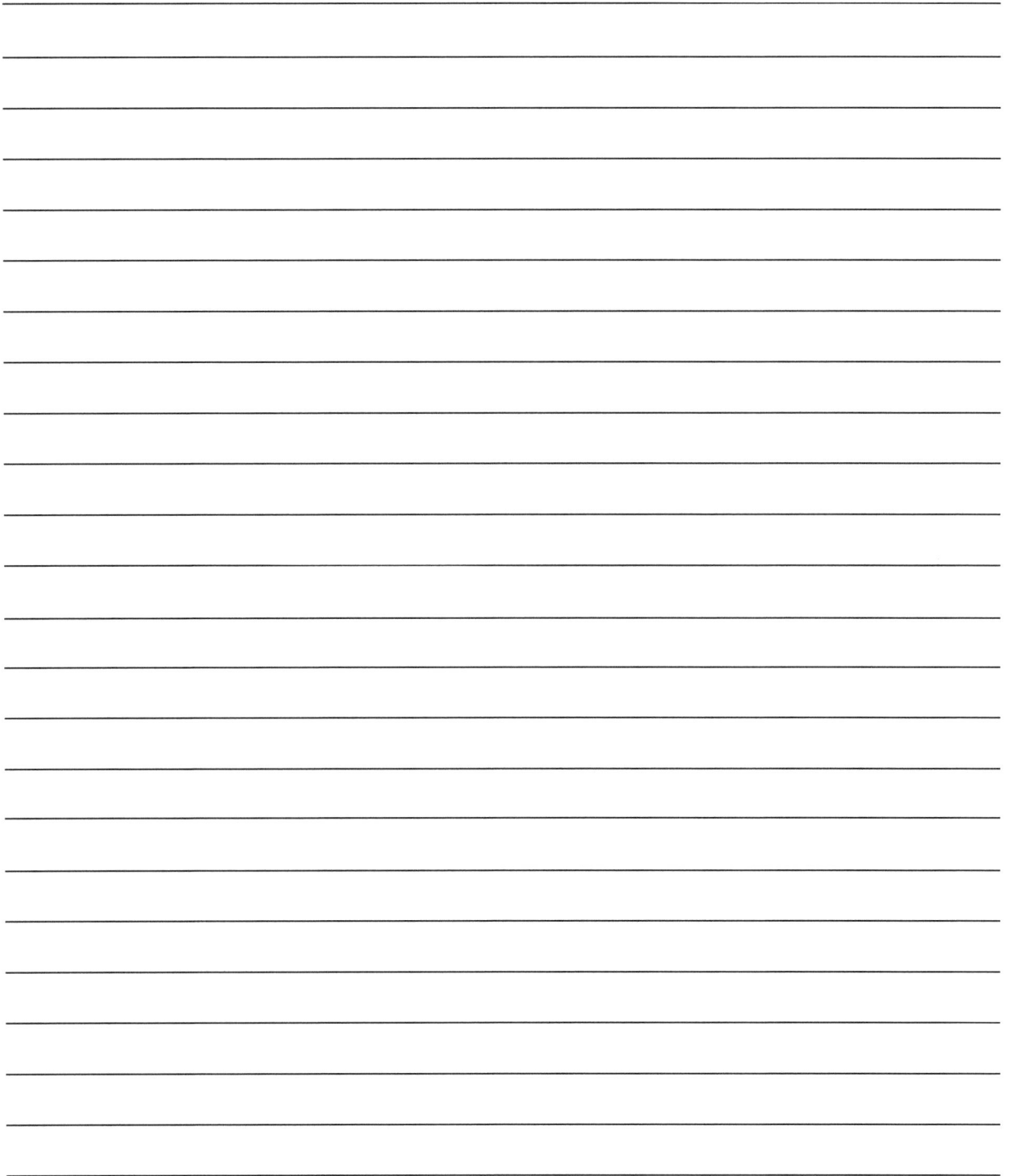

My Retirement Fun

Cheers to RETIREMENT!

My Family & Grands

Births, Memories, Plans, Photos, etc

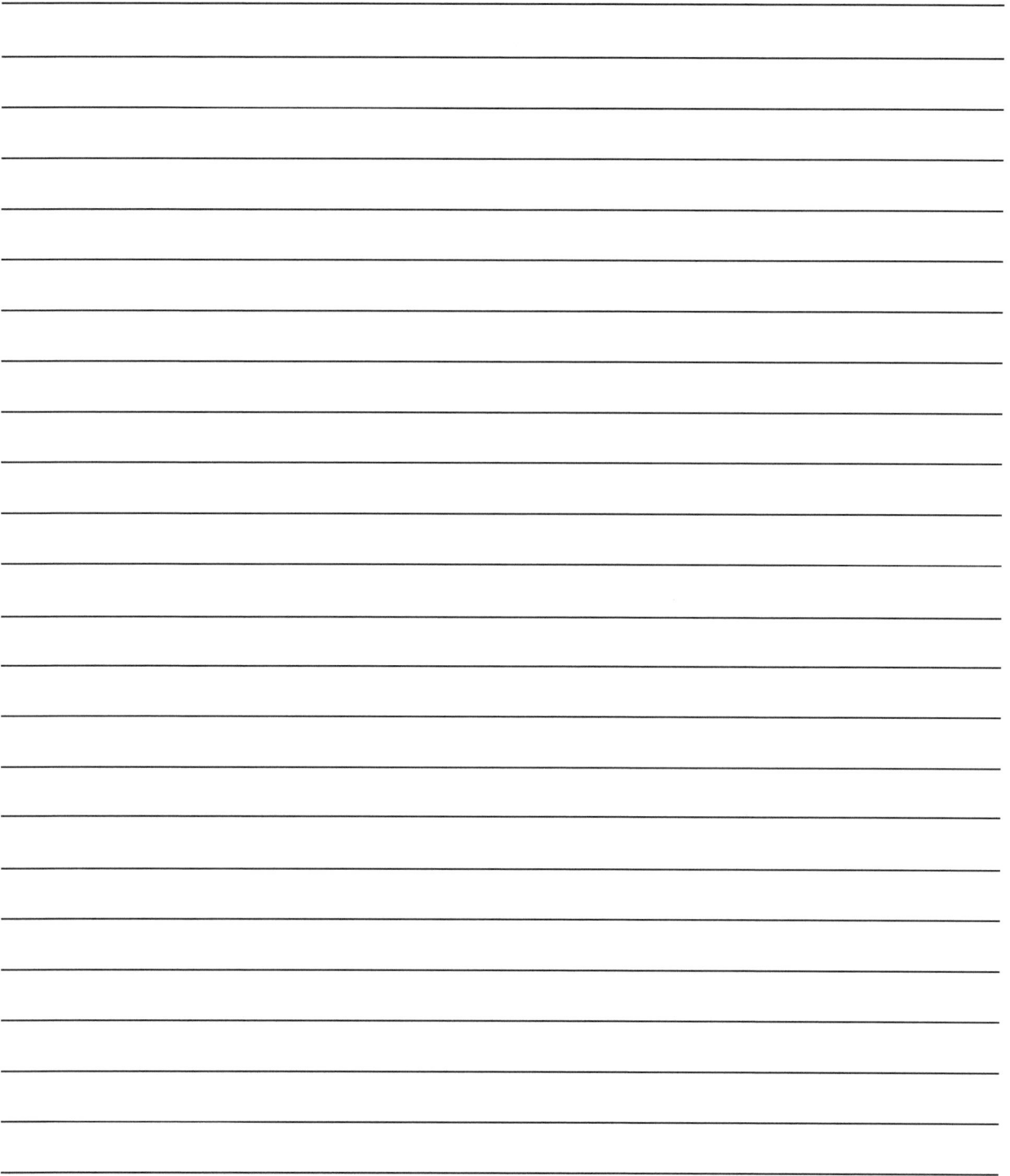

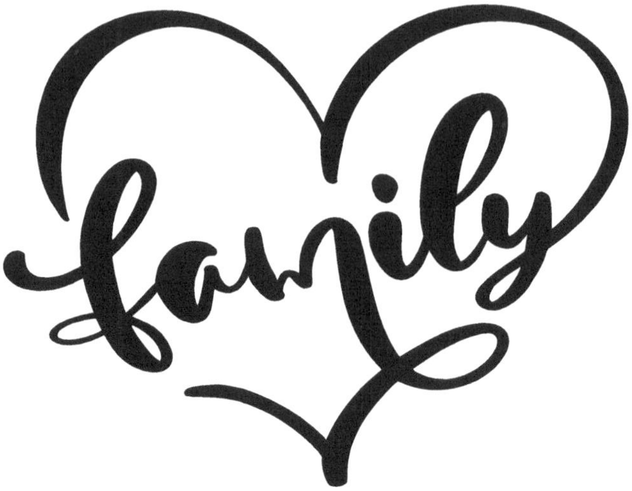
family

My Health & Wellness

Conditions, Goals, Meds, Foods, etc.

My Hobbies

Cooking, Crafts, Gardening, Reading, etc.

_____

_____

_____

_____

_____

_____

_____

_____

_____

_____

_____

_____

_____

_____

_____

_____

_____

_____

_____

_____

My Traveling Goals

Budget, Places To Go, Planning, etc.

My Family & Friends I've Lost

Cherish The Memories

_____

_____

_____

_____

_____

_____

_____

_____

_____

_____

_____

_____

_____

_____

_____

_____

_____

_____

_____

_____

_____

_____

My Special Photos

My Special Photos

My Special Photos

My Final Words & Reflections

Thoughts Of My Work Journey

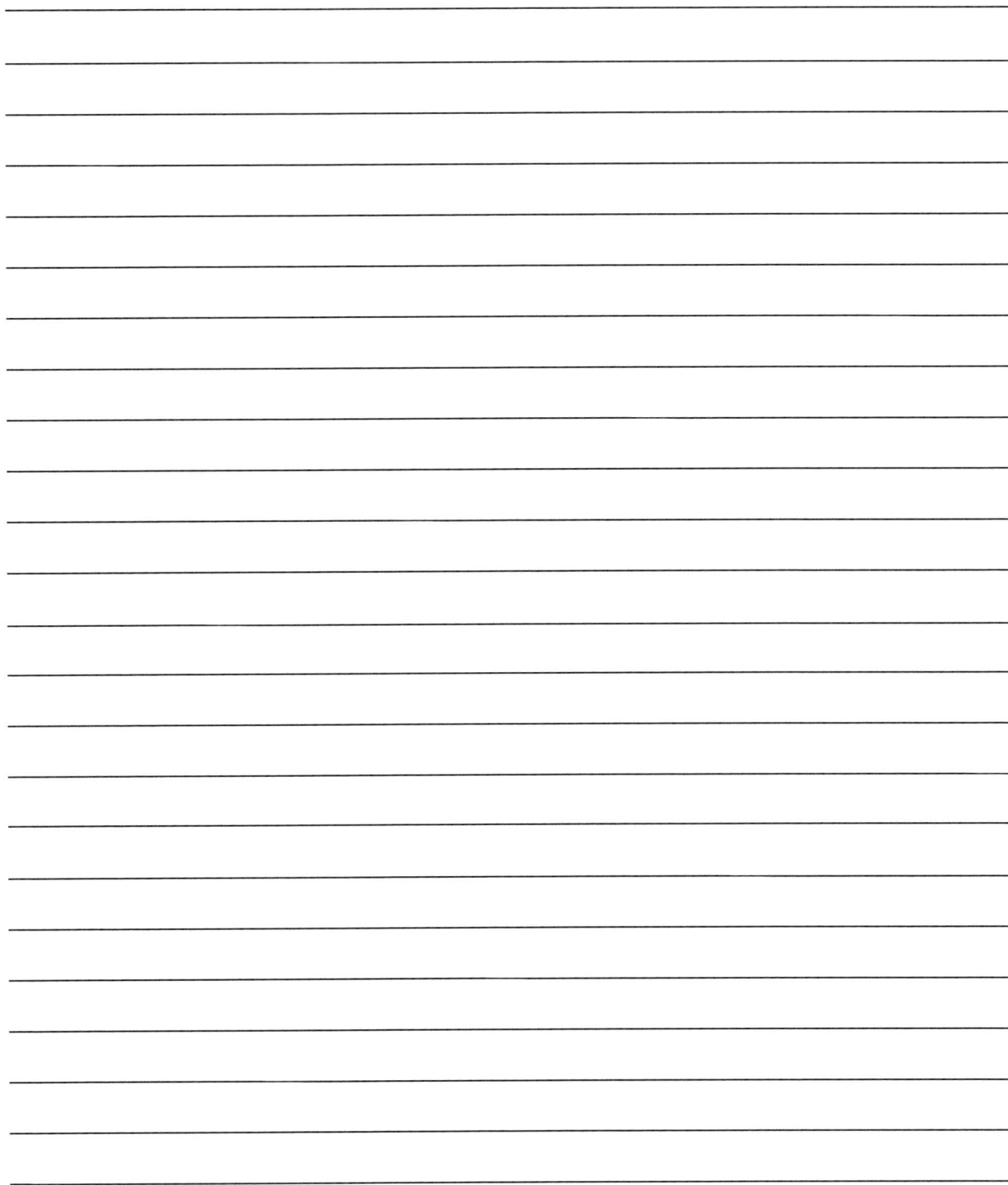

www.ingramcontent.com/pod-product-compliance
Lightning Source LLC
Chambersburg PA
CBHW061140030426
42335CB00002B/60